long i

nds & Letters 20

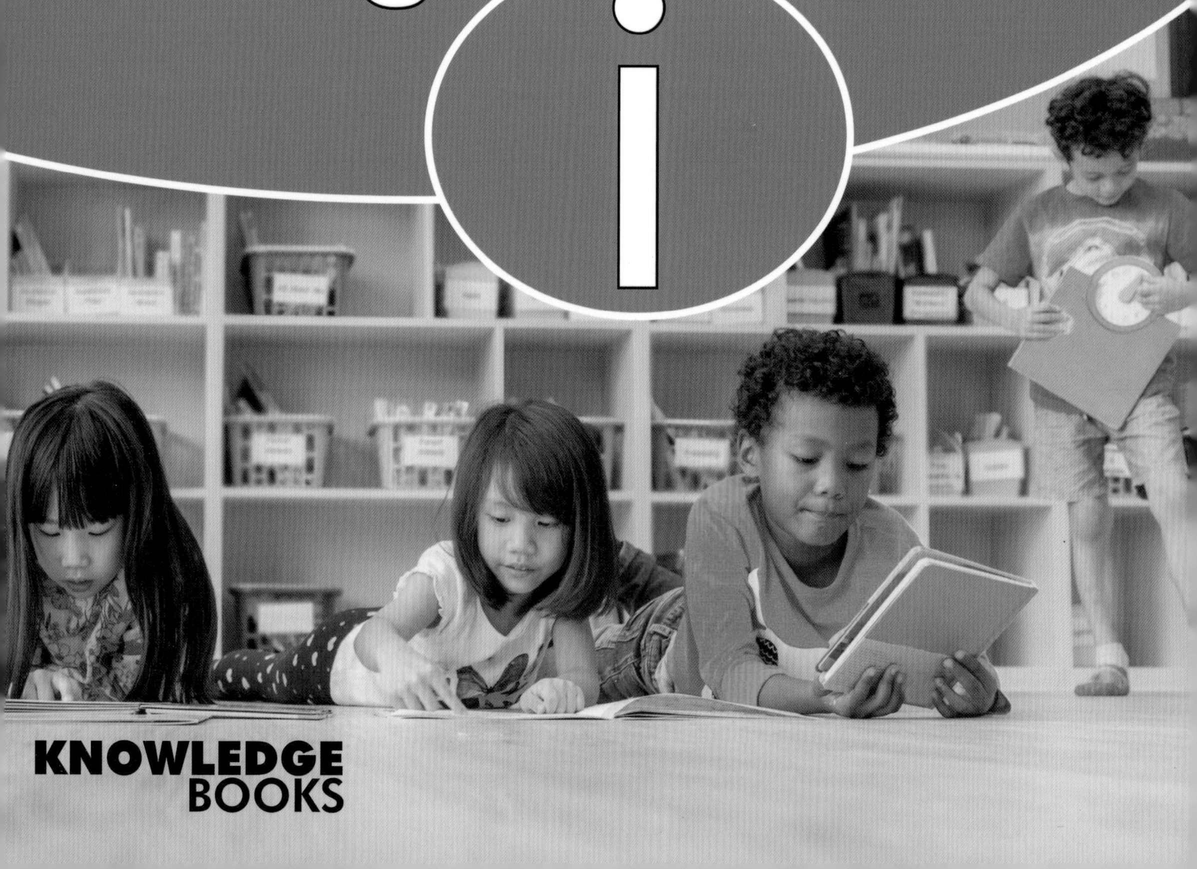

KNOWLEDGE BOOKS

bike	pie
island	light
slide	pipe
kite	

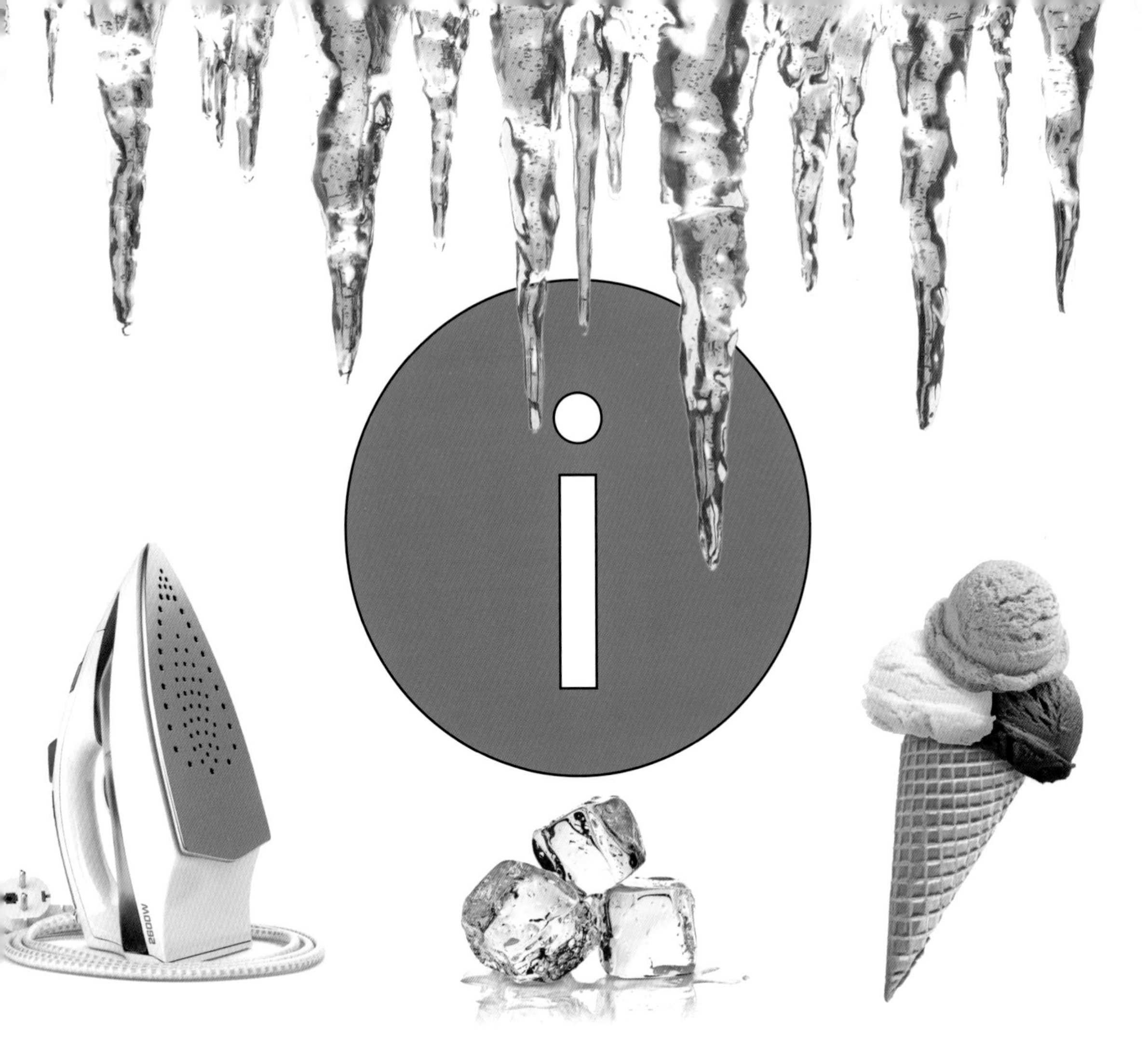

bike

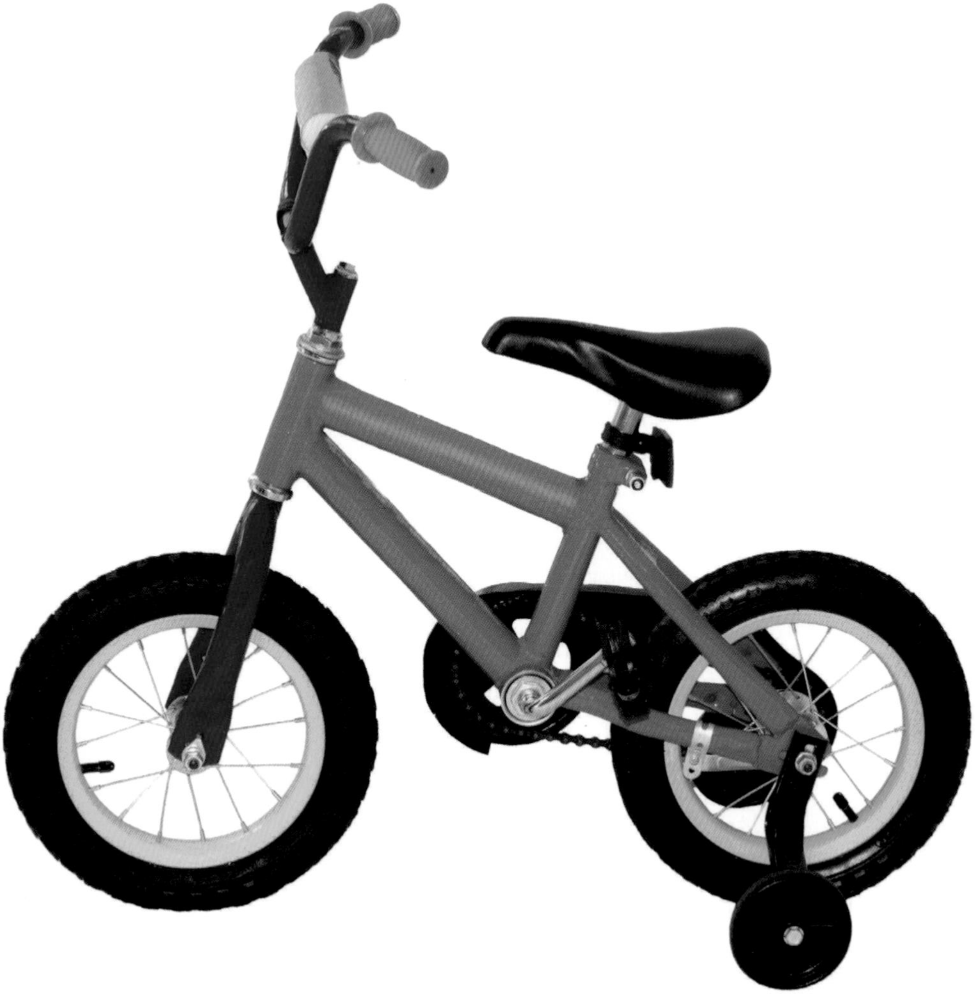

pie

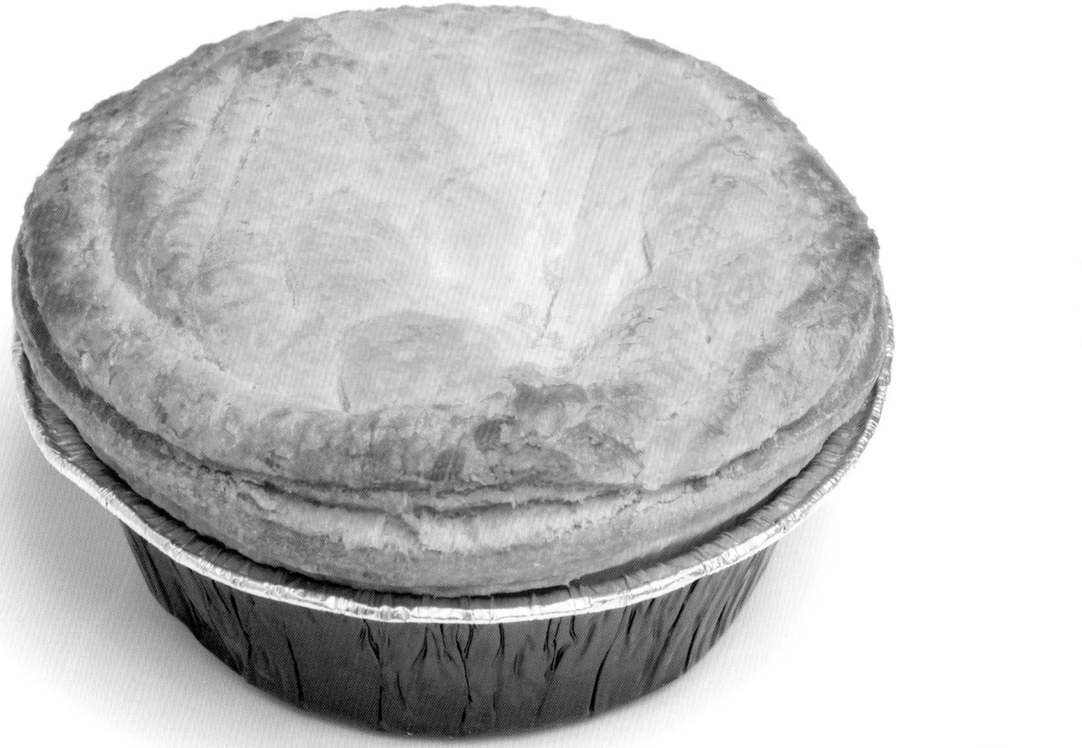

island

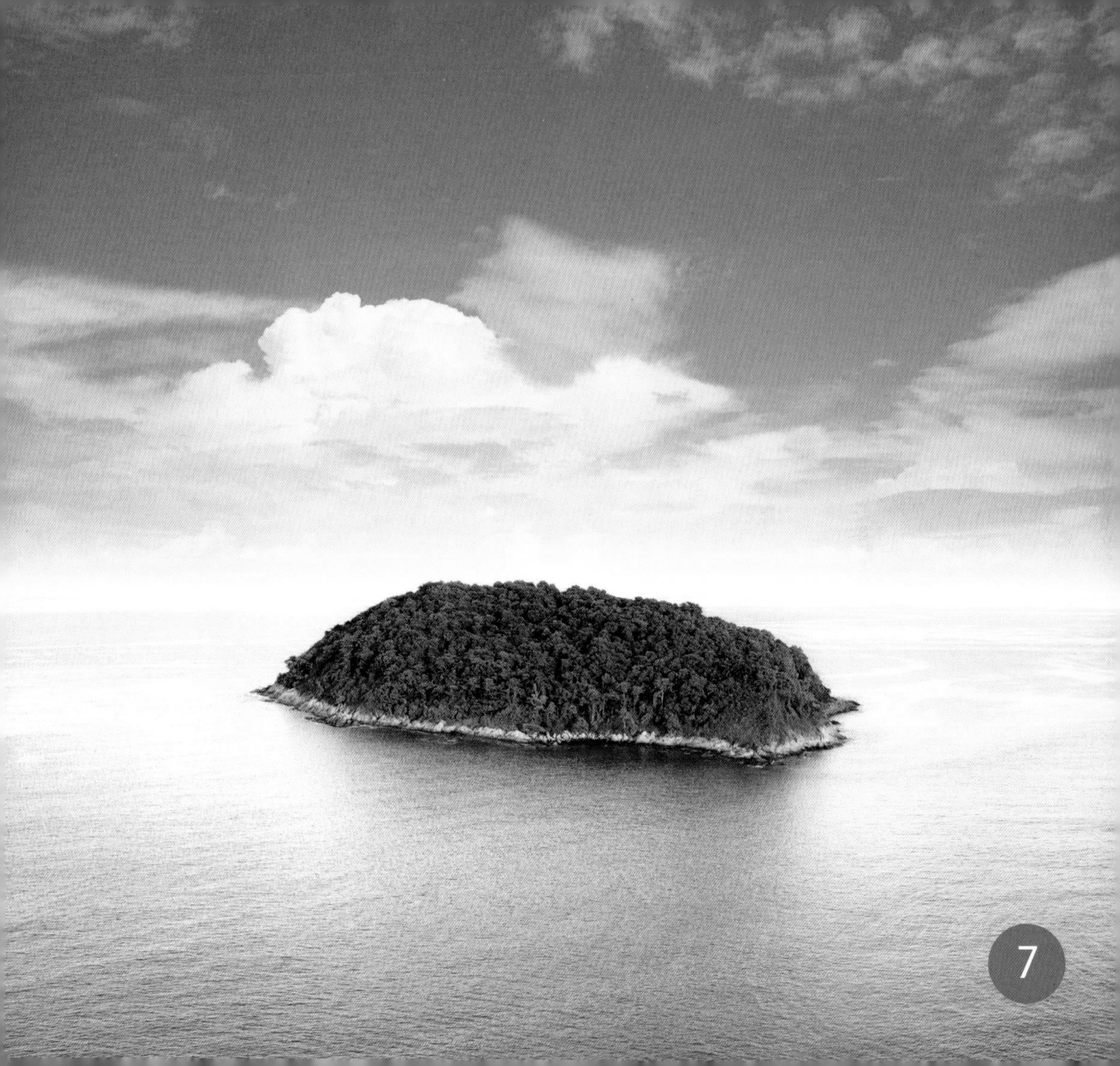

light

slide

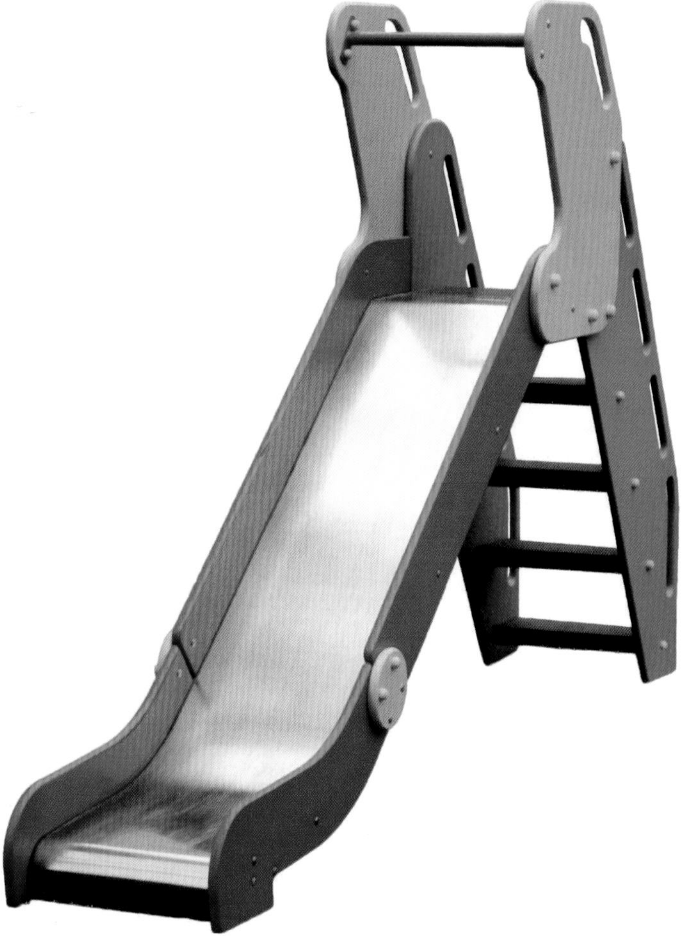

pipe

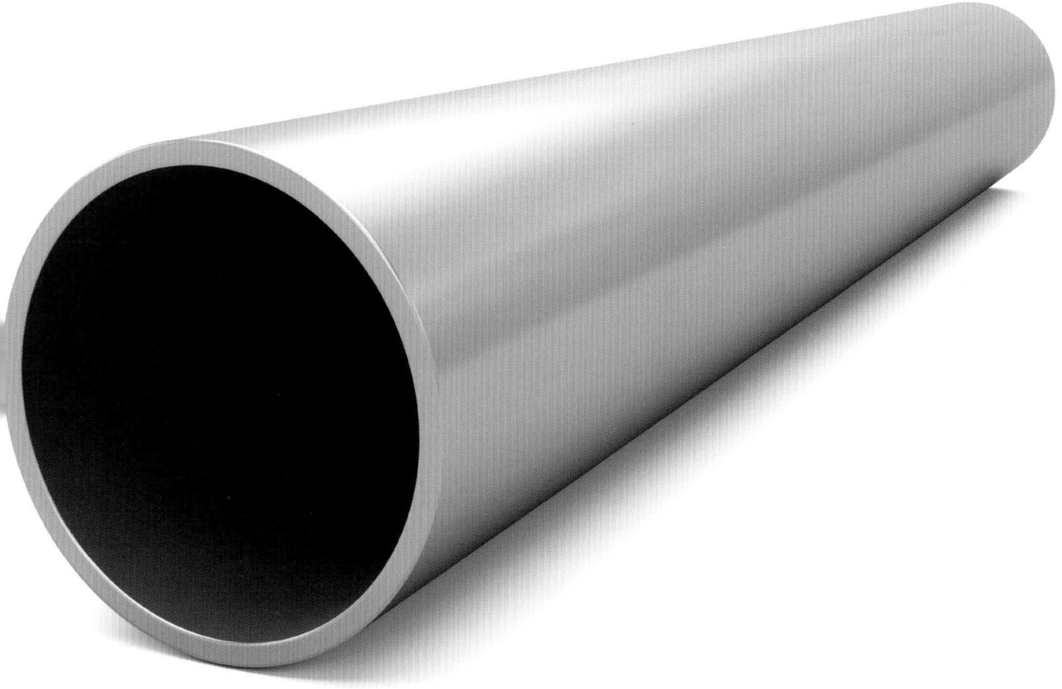

kite

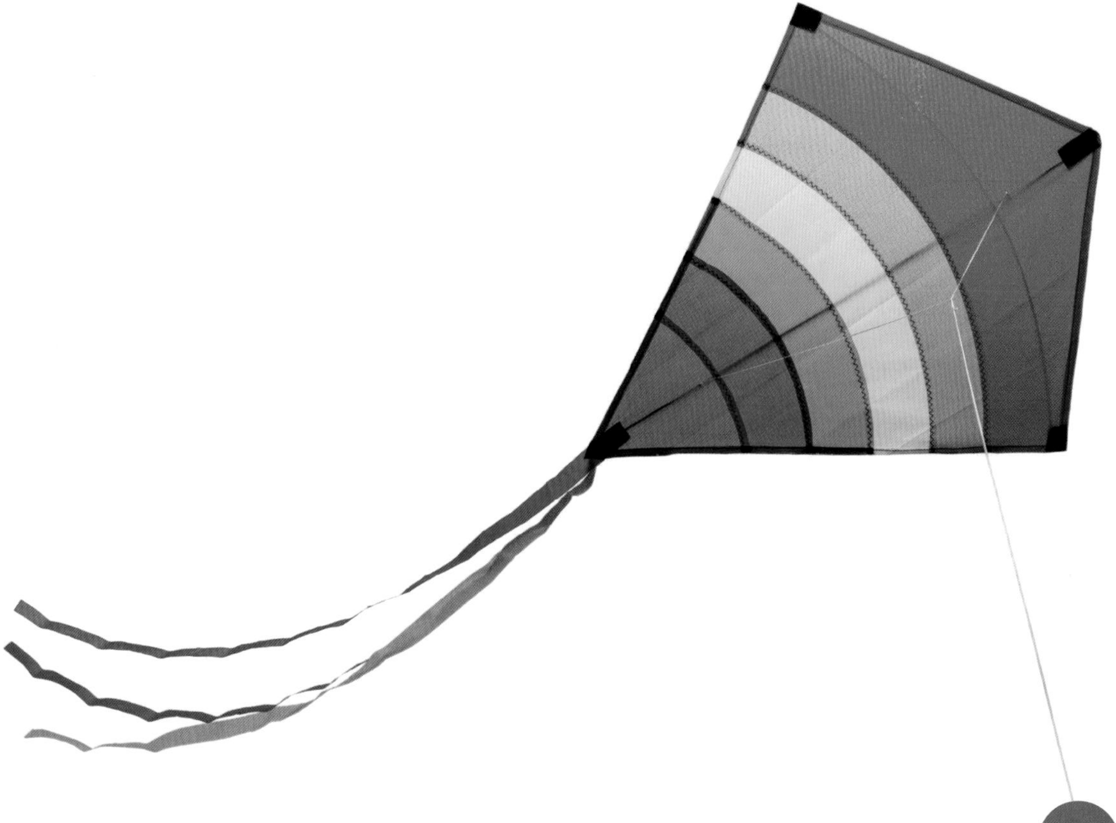

bike	pie
island	light
slide	pipe
kite	